Contents

Why are bugs poisonous?   4

Where do bugs get their poisons?   6

Fearsome fangs   8

Garden picnic   10

Poisonous claws   12

Beware of bees!   14

Wicked wasp stings   16

Stinging scorpions   18

Bug wars   20

Ant attack   22

Bubbles and blisters   24

Hairy surprises   26

Don't eat me!   28

Words to remember   30

Index   32

Why are bugs poisonous?

Some **bugs** use their nasty poisons to kill for food. Others use poisons to **defend** themselves from enemies.

This assassin bug has pumped poison into a **bee**. It then sucks up the bee's insides.

Bug Zone

Bugs

Barbara Taylor

Chrysalis Children's Books

First published in the UK in 2003 by
Chrysalis Children's Books
An imprint of Chrysalis Books Group Plc
The Chrysalis Building, Bramley Road, London W10 6SP

Paperback edition first published in 2005

ISBN 1 84138 814 9 (hb)
ISBN 1 84458 268 X (pb)

British Library Cataloguing in Publication Data
for this book is available from the British Library.

Editorial manager: Joyce Bentley
Assistant editor: Clare Chambers

Project manager and editor: Penny Worms
Designer: Angie Allison
Picture researcher: Jenny Barlow
Consultant: Michael Chinery

Printed in China
10 9 8 7 6 5 4 3 2 1

All reasonable efforts have been made to trace the relevant copyright holders of the images contained within this book. If we were unable to reach you, please contact Chrysalis Education.

B = bottom; C = centre; L = left; R = right; T = top.
Front Cover Montage (main) FLPA/B. Casals BL FLPA/C. Newton BCL FLPA/B. Casals BCR FLPA/Minden Pictures/M. Moffett BR NHPA/Anthony Bannister Back Cover L FLPA/F. Merlet R (see front cover) 1 FLPA/L. Lee Rue 4 Ecoscene/Wayne Lawler 5 (see cover) 6 FLPA/R. Planck Dembinsky 7 FLPA/E & D Hosking 8 RSPCA/Wild Images/Carol Buchanan 9 T (see cover) B FLPA/L. West 10 Papilio/Ken Wilson 11 R Photolibrary/W. B Irwin 12 and 13 RSPCA Photolibrary/Wild Images/Tim Martin 14 (see cover) 15 T FLPA/T. Davidson B FLPA/R. Wilmhurst 16 (see cover) 17 FLPA/B. Casals 18 and 19 RSPCA Photolibrary/Hans Christian Heap 20 M & P Fogden 21 OSF/Satoshi Kuribayashi 22 Natural Visions/Andrew Henley 23 OSF/Scott Camazine 24 (see cover) 25 Ecoscene/Kjell Sandved 26 RSPCA Photolibrary/Wild Images/C. Farneti Foster 27 (see 1) 28 RSPCA Photolibrary/Geoff du Feu 29 T (see cover) B RSPCA Photolibrary/Phil Bryson.

The poisons inside this cardinal **beetle's** body taste horrible.

Enemies soon learn to leave poisonous bugs alone. They will either get burned or stung, or the bug will taste really nasty.

Some of the most poisonous bugs are **spiders**, such as the funnel-web spider and the black widow spider.

Where do bugs get their poisons?

The poison made inside the black widow spider is strong enough to kill a person.

Bugs such as spiders, **wasps** and **scorpions** make poisons inside their bodies. They usually store the poison in a special **sac** until they need it.

Many **caterpillars**, **grasshoppers**, shieldbugs and beetles get their poisons from the plants that they eat.

Many shieldbugs make very smelly poisons. That's why they are nicknamed stinkbugs!

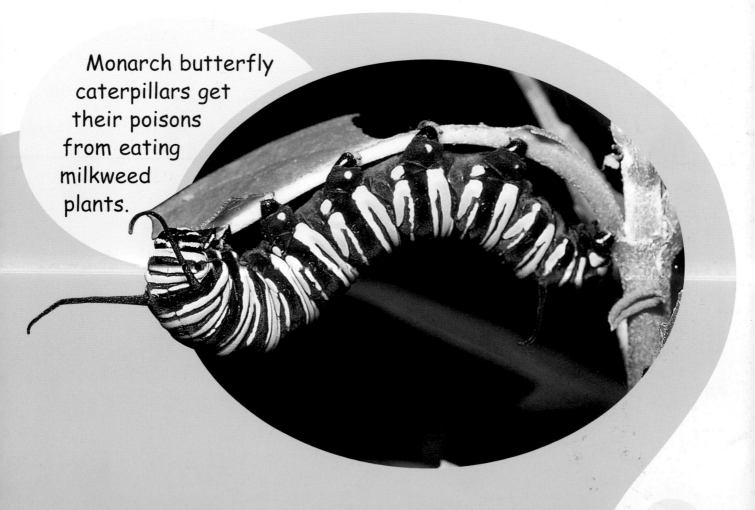

Monarch butterfly caterpillars get their poisons from eating milkweed plants.

Fearsome fangs

Spiders use their sharp **fangs** to **inject** poison into their **prey**. The poison **paralyses** or kills the prey.

A funnel-web spider's fangs are strong enough to go through your fingernail.

This funnel-web spider is showing off its huge fangs. It is saying "Keep away!"

8

This jumping spider is about to stab an **ant** with its fangs.

A spider's poison also helps to **dissolve** its prey into a mushy soup. This is useful because spiders have small mouths and cannot chew.

This jumping spider is sucking the soup from a mosquito.

Garden picnic

Even spiders you find in the garden have enough poison to kill a bug much larger than themselves, such as flies.

Spiders use their poisons to kill or paralyse other bugs quickly, before being harmed themselves.

Can you guess which is the female garden spider in this picture?

Female spiders are usually bigger and more poisonous than male spiders.

Although garden spiders can kill a fly, you would hardly notice if they bit you!

Poisonous claws

All **centipedes** have a pair of claws, which work like fangs. Centipedes stab their claws into the animals they hunt and then inject poison into the wound. Their claws are also used for defence.

Giant centipedes can give people a very painful stab with their claws but their poison does not usually kill people.

12

Giant centipedes, up to 30 cm long, live in the tropical rainforests of Central and South America. Large ones also live in Africa.

This giant centipede is busy eating a mouse for its supper.

Even small garden centipedes have poisonous claws.

Beware of bees!

Bees make their food from flowers, so they only use their poison for defence, not for catching food.

When really threatened, a bee will **sting** an attacker, injecting poison through its sting.

Only female bees can sting you. Males do not have a sting.

The bee's sting comes out of its back end. A honeybee's sting has a jagged end, like a line of tiny fishing hooks.

A honeybee's sting stays stuck in its victim's skin. This is why a honeybee can only sting once. A bumble bee can sting more than once, but is less likely to because it is not so fierce.

Birds called bee-eaters love to eat bees, but first they bash them against a branch to squeeze out the poison.

Wicked wasp stings

Wasps use their stings to defend themselves. Some wasps also sting to kill food for their young. A wasp's sting comes out of the back end of its body, just like a bee's.

Only female wasps, like these workers, can sting. Male wasps cannot sting.

This sand wasp has paralysed a caterpillar. It will become a food store for the wasp's young.

A wasp's sting is different from a honeybee's because it is smooth, so it can be pulled out of a victim and used again.

The female tarantula hawk wasp stings tarantula spiders and feeds them to her young.

stinging scorpions

A scorpion has a sharp sting at the end of its tail. It mostly uses this sting to defend itself by stabbing and injecting poison into any attacker.

Most scorpions usually kill prey with their sharp front pincers.

A scorpion's poison is in a sac at the end of its tail, next to the curved, pointed sting.

Small scorpions with weak **pincers** can use their stings to help them catch bugs as large as they are.

A scorpion can control how much poison it injects with each sting.

Bug wars

Some bugs spray their poison. Their deadly jets of stinging, burning poison gives enemies an unpleasant shock, giving the bugs time to escape.

If enemies get too close, the green lynx spider squirts a stream of poison from its fangs.

Nasute **termites** defend their nest by squirting poisonous glue at enemies out of their long, pointy snouts.

The bombardier beetle can fire its spray in almost any direction. The spray comes out with a loud POP!

The star sprayers are bombardier beetles. They mix up poisons inside their bodies to make a boiling hot spray, which they squirt out of their back end.

Ant attack

This Australian bulldog ant is stinging a wasp. The sting is at the back end of its body, linked to a sac of poison.

Many kinds of ant have a sting to inject their poisons. The sting is smooth, like a wasp sting, and can be used again and again.

The fire ants of the Americas are named after their painful sting, which burns the skin.

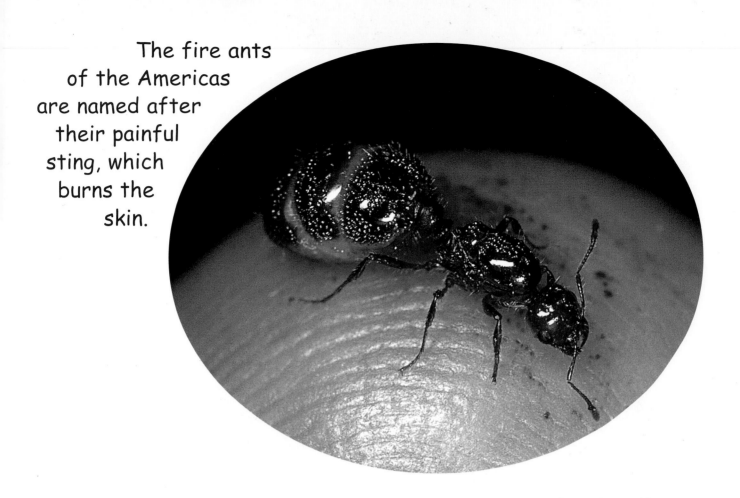

Some ants spray poisonous acid at their enemies. The acid burns and makes the eyes water so enemies cannot see.

Some rainforest ants use their poison to protect their tree homes from harm by other creatures.

23

Bubbles and blisters

Some bugs don't have fangs, claws or stings to inject their poison. They don't spray it either.

This young foam **locust** is oozing smelly, poisonous bubbles for protection while it feeds.

This leafhopper is giving off drops of two different poisons – a clear one from its back end and a white one along its side.

Instead, their poisons just leak out of their bodies as bubbles or drops.

Both blister beetles and **ladybirds** leak poisonous blood from their knees.

Hairy surprises

Don't touch the poisonous spines of the Saddleback caterpillar!

Did you know that some hairy caterpillars can sting you? They have hollow hairs, linked to sacs of poison, which they use for defence. When the hairs are touched, they release the poison.

The
tarantula's
prickly hairs
are on its
back.

The tarantula spider has
another hairy surprise. If attacked,
it flicks prickly hairs at its enemy,
using its back legs.

Tarantula hairs
are coated with
poison. They stick in
the skin and cause a
painful rash.

Don't eat me!

A ladybird's colours warn other bugs that it tastes nasty.

You may have noticed by now that poisonous bugs are often brightly coloured. Bright colours are in fact a clue to whether a bug is poisonous or not.

Non-poisonous bugs sometimes copy the warning colours of poisonous bugs. This tricks enemies into leaving them alone.

A ladybird spider has the same red and black warning colours as a ladybird.

Bright colours on a bug are called **warning colours**. They mean "I taste nasty. Don't eat me".

This burnet **moth** flies during the daytime but is safe because of its bright warning colours.

ant A small insect that lives with other ants in a large group called a colony.

bee A flying insect that usually feeds its young pollen and nectar from flowers. It usually has a sting.

beetle A flying insect with tough front wings that cover most of the body like a case.

bug A true bug is a type of insect with a stabbing beak. The word 'bug' is now used to mean any type of minibeast.

caterpillar A young butterfly or moth.

centipede A long minibeast (not an insect) with many legs and poisonous claws.

defence A way of protecting oneself from enemies or rivals.

dissolve To turn into a liquid.

fang Sharp, pointed mouthparts used to inject poison into prey or enemies.

grasshopper A jumping insect with long, powerful back legs. It usually has wings too.

inject To make a hole in the skin to push another liquid into the body.

insect A minibeast with three parts to its body and six legs. Most insects can fly.

ladybird A type of small beetle, usually red with black spots.

locust A type of grasshopper.

moth A flying insect that usually flies at night and is a dull colour.

paralyse To make something unable to move.

pincers Large claws that grip together.

prey An animal that is killed or eaten by another animal.

sac A place where poison is stored.

scorpion A minibeast (not an insect) with two big claws and a powerful sting in its tail.

spider A minibeast (not an insect) with eight legs and two poisonous fangs.

sting A sharp, pointed tube, like a needle, used to inject poison.

termite A small insect, similar to an ant, that lives in huge nests containing thousands, even millions, of termites.

warning colours The bright colours of a bug, which warn attackers that it might bite, sting or taste nasty.

wasp A flying insect that uses its sting to kill other bugs.

Index

ants 9, 22-23, 30

assassin bug 4

bees 4, 14-15, 30

beetles 5, 7, 21, 25, 28, 30

caterpillars 7, 17, 26, 30

centipedes 12-13, 30

claws 12-13

fangs 8-9, 12, 20, 30

grasshoppers 7, 30

hairs 26-27

inject 8, 12, 18, 19, 22, 30

ladybirds 25, 28, 31

leafhopper 25

locust 24, 31

moth 29, 31

paralyse 8, 10, 17, 31

sac 6, 19, 22, 26, 31

scorpions 6, 18-19, 31

shieldbugs 7

smell (poisonous) 7, 24

spiders 5, 6, 8-9, 10-11, 17, 20, 27, 29, 31

spray (poisonous) 20-21, 23

sting 14-19, 22-23, 26, 31

termites 20, 31

warning colours 28-29, 31

wasps 6, 16-17, 22, 31